Lauds

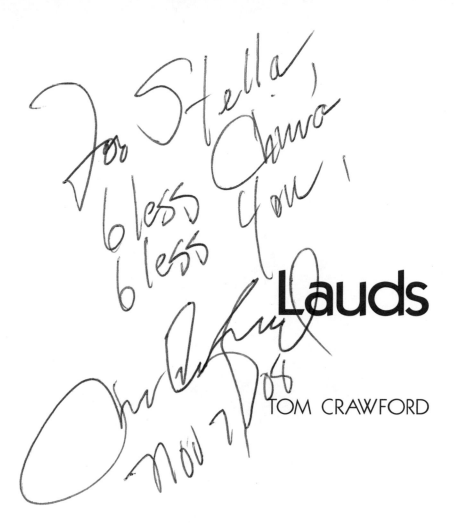

For Stella,
bless Anna
bless You !
bless

[signed] Tom Crawford
Nov 7 2006

Lauds

TOM CRAWFORD

Cedar House Books
Seattle, Washington

Acknowledgments are due to the editors of the following, in
which some of these poems have appeared:

*Poetry East, Fireweed, Calapooya, Life on the Line, A
Gathering of Poets, A New Geography of Poets, The Malahat
Review, Handspan of Red Earth*

also...

The author wishes to thank
the National Endowment for the Arts
for its generous support.

დ

CONTENTS

17 ARS POETICA

SECTION I

21 GRETEL 1.

22 GRETEL 2.

23 GRETEL 3.
(Some Recent Criticism)

25 GRETEL 4.

26 WATER OUZEL

27 BEGIN WITH WHAT'S CONSTANT

29 WAVE

31 PILOT WHEEL COTTAGES

32 FARMER CREEK

34 TREES

36 LAST SALMON

37 CRACKED CORN

38 MAPLE

40 LETTER FROM A PSYCHIC

41 THE TOLL BIRDS TAKE

43 SONG OF THE CARPENTER

45   OTIS CAFE

47   ANAGAMA

49   THE LONGING

50   AZURE

SECTION II

52   TRAPPIST ABBEY
OUR LADY OF GUADALUPE,
LAFAYETTE, OREGON

SECTION III

63   PRAYER

64   A CHANCE TO TRAVEL

66   THE WAR EFFORT, 1945

67   BOMBER PILOT

70   UNTITLED

72   AUTUMN

73   SALMON

74   AUTUMN IN AMERICA

76   PUMPKIN

77   DOGWOOD

78   IN PRAISE OF THE LIGHT

80   THE FRANKLIN EXPEDITION 1855

82   MARRIAGE

83 SNOW

84 THE HEART

85 MY FATHER'S HANDS

87 KEEPSAKE

88 GRANDFATHER

90 WASHING

Try to be an ear,
and if you do speak, ask for explanations.

— RUMI

For my best friend, Krissy

ARS POETICA

They are what we have,
the dead
and their words,
precise as cut flowers
The light in the jar
that won't go out
The names we take to heart
through all our travail

— TOM CRAWFORD

SECTION I

GRETEL
1.

Don't say, "Who can understand
this life," and mean the oatmeal
or the whole milk
and butter it swims in
I was out walking this morning
after breakfast
in my rubber boots
with my old goat. Gretel
could still win best-of-show
just for showing up
and for the shape of her udder
Attachment *is* what you look for
in a goat
when you're judging
and we love our walk together
down to the creek
through the wet pasture
Light, everywhere, is an appointment
we should keep
when we are quiet
enough, and can find the path

GRETEL
2.

We are like two old miners
Gretel, you and I,
far from the world
working, as best we can, this claim
we have on each other
For the poet and his goat
no day is ordinary
the way we love to eat
our way through
what light has given
The branch of sweet elderberry
you can't reach
I pull down
It's that kind of relationship
when words mean less
than leaves
which your long, black tongue
curls around, another morning
we don't pay Caesar's taxes
Nothing lost then_what color is
to invention
A red plane scoots over the trees
now, and disappears

For Thomas McGrath

GRETEL (Some Recent Criticism)
3.

Dear Thomas, I fed you to my goat
on Memorial Day, Monday, well, not you exactly
but those mostly well-mannered poets
toward the back of the book
she turned down, *flat*
the way I knew she would
Gretel, when she can choose,
prefers skunk cabbage or thistle
Goats love best the volunteer
what comes up cross
out of the ground
It's the sour breath of the good poem she longs for
when she makes her rounds
Wild cucumber, for example, will shut your mouth
so fast, or mine, but Gretel
rolls in the bitter vines
with one consummate gesture of tongue
those spotted green tubular growths
and spiny leaves go down
and if there were an American flag tied to the end
we would lose our country
Goats don't understand pretense
the way they eat to live
the gluey wrapper around a tin can
the off-set print of Campbell Soup

Bly survived
It may have been, as much as anything,
where he fell
in this issue of taste I'm telling you about
Goats everywhere in the world
are a test of any poem
dropped off there
on the bleakest islands they survive
Shot back to a lonely pair
by the U.S. Navy on the Farallons
they came back eating stinging nettle
and fucking together another bearded world
of hybrid vigor and hoof-rot
"That a poem in some way stink, is what I look for,"
Pound must have said

I lied about giving Gretel the book
She took it
You were what was missing

GRETEL

4.

There's nothing wrong with your legs
but I'll rub in the liniment anyway
knowing all along that you've decided
the way a goat will
to die just because
and nothing can tempt you back
not even the wind and new fall
of sweet leaves along the creek.
Astronomy is what I'm left
with you bony old goat
in a field of white stars
burned out
across a void that weighs like grief
I'll say your name.
And in the pasture, in the months to come,
I'll stop over the gray droppings,
a dumb poet
who's on to nothing,
still attached to the ordinary.

WATER OUZEL

Maybe it's from moss he gets the green light to walk
under water. In Paul's letter to the Ephesians he's
almost mentioned, but who would believe in the
miracle of a little bird especially standing in white
water peering down around his own feet for food
while the creek flows over. "Down there" is always
subjective, but you can watch him descend in a zig-
zag walk down to where light sets the table. Small
himself, it's the spineless he's after. What we want
to figure out, he eats. How many feet of creek does it
take, for example, to make one Ouzel? What feeling
is to poetry, larvae to caddis — a sudden hatch —
the porch light by the screen door where hundreds
hang on. We have to be content to name what he
brings up: hellgrammite, nymph, stonefly.

For Doug Haga

BEGIN WITH WHAT'S CONSTANT

Begin with what's constant,
this life, to be loved
hands down
deep inside my pockets,
the long, quiet walk out
on a beach strewn with agates
and old people
bent over, carrying their little plastic bags
to collect them
Where the Herring gull,
who is larger than the rest
claims the dead snapper
with the eyeless head
(more fish than ever now)
filleted out to bone
from some boat far off shore
that follows the same old rule
"We all have to eat."
Color should be enough, I say to red sky
and a washed up bullwhip

❧ ∽ ❧

I know better
the years of good luck and drift
before I could say a word
I was one in the photograph,
sand sticking to my fat cheeks
sitting between my mother's legs
on Long Beach in California
Nothing has changed: the poet in diapers,
in the background a steady line of waves
breaking in black and white
It's wrong to want more or less
than what the sea brings in
The red catsup bottle is an example
of what I mean
or the saw-log from Coos Bay
that did nothing more than follow the current
I love the immutable law of fade
and goodby,
the sunset wash
in a world I can wave to

WAVE

The idiot who keeps pointing
has something to say

Turn away . . . you missed it
The enormous whale slips under the surface again
not 100 yards from where you're standing

Close your eyes for a moment
and your name
in tow
on the horizon
turns back
into an ordinary ship
you feel comfortable with

Listen!

Every wave holds up something: the sun
in miniature
the truth, a reflection
which always bends toward you
concave
and beautiful coming in

Cold November, the beach littered with dead
        Murres
The one helpless gull with the broken wing
who wanders off
ahead of you

O aimless waves
that are always breaking
on what shore
you call home

PILOT WHEEL COTTAGES

There was an ocean view on June 11, too (1940), and reasonable rates. Almost before you were in the world. A couple rented one of the red cottages for a weekend of love-making and long walks on the beach and him outside the bedroom window, not to look at her (Rosalie) taking off her clothes but because it was dark enough back there and private that he could blissfully aim his penis at the clapboard and let go. The pleasure of sound, wave on wave, and piss mixing it all up: Pilot Wheel Cottages, that's the letterhead (yellow now) Edward G. Smith used, Proprietor, it says, to write down his horrors of the coming war, "The Germans are within 25 miles of Paris . . . ," and seal it with a copy of a daily paper in the cottage wall. How the lovers must have moved on the sheets that night, allies to the oldest cause, fingers digging in, scattering the pillows. From where they were lying below the window sash they couldn't see the horizon or the three ships steaming north. To Puget Sound. The navy yards. Young men aboard, excited, anxious for liberty (Who read books then?) spit-shining their black shoes. Edward G. Smith is dead by now. His fears, everything else remains, lovely, the ocean view with its red dress flying.

FARMER CREEK

If I were an Indian I could call on the creek for a
vision, get the salmon to talk and not just stink until
Farmer Creek floats the dead ones down to the
Nestucca. The big male hanging over the vine maple
gets riper by the day. He's old now and coming out
of his clothes. When the water began to drop after
the early November storm, he couldn't break loose.
Now each day more of him shows. At first I could
just see the dark back and fin. But after four days (I
come out every morning, coffee cup in hand, in my
rubber boots) he is fully exposed, hanging, U-
shaped, tail and head swinging into each other.
Eyes opaque. It's a kind of fiction right here in my
backyard, the hero, after a long and dangerous
journey, comes home to die. My uncle Oscar
crashed his B-17, it's assumed, somewhere in the
New Guinea jungle. One of those dreary
reconnaissance flights. Bad weather. He probably
ran out of gas. Where's the glory? The party home?
That's him now in his black shirt. He must have
swelled up in the cockpit and stank like this in the
plane the crew named *Papa's Waltz*. Where was
Farmer Creek in 1943? Not in uniform or aiming a
gun, that's for sure. A creek can compromise. That's
the thing. Take on anyone's name. Right now it's
Farmer Creek, America. A good place to fish. The
blue heron who always lands quietly down by the
bridge then walks up toward the house along the
bank, intent, taking its sweet time, knows that.

Eleven years I've lived here. The dogwood I planted this spring took root. I've been sleeping sounder lately. Last night I had this wonderful dream, in color. People introduced themselves. It was raining.

TREES

I like thinking about who thought them up
in the first place
and could figure in the wind
and rocky soil
with plans, all along, for birds
and a green horizon, then said,
"Grow here," the first tent,
pitched the old way, to stay put
when that might have saved them.

In the kingdom of roots
we have to imagine a future
which may not include us,
where everything of ours is thrown out
in the rain: the rose cup
and saucer,
our neatly folded t-shirts,
you name it, all mixed up
in the dirt, in the rain.

If we had only been raised to sit still
awhile, just not move
where the creek slows, then divides
to flow past the "blow down,"
and had learned to dip our arms, every day,
into the cold water
until we *could not stand it,* every day,
if we had done that,
alone.

After each storm
isn't there always the quiet interlude
when the heavy sky lifts
and when the last rain forms into slow drops
along the eaves
or drips from the leaves?
We know this place,
this soft light — the heart opening — a small room
in the world.

LAST SALMON

What to say about Christmas
your dying gift to the world
which requires your whole body
become a black shovel
all week in the creek behind the house
you dig, here, no here. Then settle
on the deeper, quiet water
below the cedar

Isn't the world almost perfect
that we don't have to choose
between the verb and its object
St. Paul or sister fish, who's doing what
to whom, in principle, always comes back
to water and ordinary light
It's enough to stand still
if we mean it, the way a tree says, *here*
then grows

CRACKED CORN

From my front porch in winter
I throw a little cracked corn to the world
Who can beat the sparrows in
all flit and scatter and return
pecking their way around the feet
of the domestics: chickens, ducks and the big
　　　bombers
our geese who come rolling up, mostly to bully
There are pleasures in distribution
where the leaves may fall
the assignment of heron to water
beside the house
My love of windows, this habit
of looking out I have, now into cold February
Who can imagine a better life?
The day, quiet, just invented
The start of crocus

MAPLE

Here is the best we can do: I'll bet
one dead Harding against your Polk
that in the nature of things
only color will last past autumn
The oldest elections on record
are fossils laid down behind the high school
gymnasium
when they were up-start, leaves
A fond wave from the tree
(Oh pure light!)
is all the history we'll get

❦

The vine maple by the creek beats
the top of the water
now that the rains have come
beats the top of the water
The creek doesn't know it's being played
by a low branch all afternoon
Doesn't know it's water
moving water and red leaves

❧

Absolution
I unlace my shoes in front of these trees
and lean back in the chair
For awhile the old noise stops
Nothing is random (that sad word)
the crow just landed
now folding its wings
is primary cause for joy
In this sunlight black comes closer
and red to what I mean

LETTER FROM A PSYCHIC

Trees still grow
and green is the dominant color
where we live
It's not that bad being dead
Most of us don't even leave town
Decisions are in the hands of just a few
we never see
and the old rule still applies: first feelings
then algebra
If you want a river, it's there
or your favorite birds
but no one is saying suffer
Death *is* tidy (our little joke)
We are all asked to take notes
and keep our rooms clean
We're supposed to see through nature
on good days
we get out just like you
We dress up for the flowers

THE TOLL BIRDS TAKE

You have to understand the toll birds take
perched or on the wing
concentrated beauty is a war of nerves
One can enter you from any direction
and a fly-through
even by the Common Sparrow
can take out the heart
That's the nature of ambush
something that lies in wait: a Nuthatch
walking perpendicular
down a tree
dressed to kill
ruined me for several years
Now I take precautions: cover my eyes
to the Wood-Duck,
stand back from the window in winter
when the Chickadees come to feed
Snow is a bad thing where any birds gather
so much color is always a show of force
Look at the ancient Crow
a black glove on the landscape
one finger always mocking you
He was ugly, but when Herby Pool stood up in class
in the eighth grade
and imitated the songs of several birds
including the difficult Vireo
we were never the same
That was years ago and he died
Don't birds die

birds above all things
who unnerve us just in passing
who leave us breathless and sad?

SONG OF THE CARPENTER

On its own
the lacy Hemlock
would never become trim
to wrap a door or a window
or Fir
a bearing wall
to hold up the roof
we live under
but where we seldom pray
If I were God
I wouldn't answer my prayers
either
which want only a good set of plans
something approved of, the world
plumb
and square
These are the problems: if we would just get the
        wind
to settle down somewhere
Or how to get rid of the useless knot
or the conniving sliver?
Cedar's too weak, you know, for framing
and under the skin it festers
Right now, in fact, I have one
in my thumb
which I can't get out — so what's it good for?
See, God, how ordinary are my petitions:
everything measured
a lock on the door

I'm still trying to separate the light
from the window —
what's mine
what's yours

OTIS CAFE

You can believe in the eight plastic hands —
    feminine
that never tire of serving
while blue saucers and chocolate donuts
spill forever down the yellow wall in front of you
a greeting to COME IN
A restaurant where you might think
what's best is nothing new: old photos
curling away from the walls
of dead loggers and fishermen, stumpage and gill
    nets
the camera couldn't lie about
and their wives, resigned, who never entered the
    picture
though they stood there, though you know they
    cooked
You have to go back in time to order your food here,
the building clapboard
and grandfathered in to an ancient grill and two
    mud roads
that diverged in a wilderness
the loudest sound then, wind through tall trees
Be sentimental
The booths give you the privacy of history
honey-grained wood and light through the window
are a way in
and if you get loud so is the kitchen loud
It's emotional to cook here or to eat
the German potatoes and black mushrooms

and not feel something: civility, the affection of
    soup?
A country built on a hustle and a sneer?
Doesn't longing keep us all a little hungry
the waitress taller (the height she wanted to be),
the nose not so squat
When it rains here the windows fog over
and if it weren't for the black coffee
in front of you, steaming, you'd want to leave,
you'd think that you had dreamed this all up

ANAGAMA

Nine miles out of Willamina
(is all I'll say) it's wild country
Turn right at the coyote
Ash fires the hole-in-the-hill
gang to come here on a Sunday
road weary from far away
Sedona, Kansas City, Norway
with their half-baked ideas
hand thrown and emotional
vessels you really can't drink out of
This is an old Biblical score
they're trying to settle
with water, a hunch, some clay
Don, I know, kisses his hand
then spits on his desert pot
before putting it in the kiln
What is faith anyway? Looking up
a pair of green mallards
take aim at the pond behind us
our perfect counterpart. Clay
gives back more than we are
if we're lucky. It mimes us.
My own comic mask comes out
not so funny. One eye hole melts
down on a cracked jaw stubbled with ash
And who can account for the rosy
horses in Jenny's porcelain? Still warm,
it helps us all just to hold them,
to be here. That's it, isn't it,

we're an old crew now
(Who sleeps anymore?)
throwing the wood on all night
pushing ourselves toward what city?

For Frank Boyden

THE LONGING

Clay is trying to be something
we only started, a grudge we have
against the ordinary
To bow well is always to bend
from the inside like a good bowl
to praise the clay, its emptiness,
the sun going down there, a black soup
we lift to our lips, the only animal who can
Or clay is an opinion we have
about ourselves which keeps on changing
and always has something to do
with gravity, we suspect
the longing that keeps us all here
pulling on our pants
and gargling to save our receding gums
while our pots sit on the shelves
squat, determined, our pals
The riverbank is as close as we can get
to the old neighborhood,
the clay we grew up in
gouged out and squished through our fingers
to make, right there, the clumsy animals
we loved. Dogs who couldn't keep their legs on,
the impossible tails. Then we knew everything:
the fun of tossing them all back
out into the deep place
to let the water take them

AZURE

Dear Sarah, today I put on your father's socks,
the blue ones you brought back from Tennessee
after he died, not necessarily to remind us we
would too. He was tired, that's all. Bill, my step-
father, who I've told you about, smoked two packs
of Camels a day and left behind his railroad watch.
An old gold-plated Hamilton which, before she
died, my mother handed to me. "Carry it son," she
said, "Bill would want that." Hazel, my sick Rhode
Island Red, sailed off last night under the towel I
put over her, it was so cold. She didn't tell me what
to do with the nine brown eggs she left behind.
What *are* we to do? The monks at Guadalupe face
each other every day and sing the same song, Lord
have mercy. It's like the rain, unlooked for,
streaking the window right now, and we need it.
Me, I cry about almost everything: light through the
glass doors, my old cat with half his teeth gone, the
smell of geraniums. In the other room Ella
Fitzgerald is singing "Azure." I've turned it up so
you can hear it, too, wherever you are. Sarah, sing
with me.

SECTION II

TRAPPIST ABBEY

OUR LADY OF GUADALUPE, LAFAYETTE, OREGON

1.

Nothing much happens here
in the routine of faith
unless it's baseball
on the one day a year all the monks retreat
farther up the hill
No planes take off here
to a straight mile of red lights, blinking
Community means something: when Fr. Peter lost
part of his thumb everybody prayed
for the gift of what remains
the ragged salad and say-grace
that dinner always brings

2.

I've always believed the soul was small,
tentative,
something *you* filled in
if you wanted,
a flower in any case
dark with a long shelf life
My guess (the monks have taught me this)
is as good as anyone's and reason enough
to retreat
Looking in, the lamp warms me
There's a small desk, a bed,
a place for my shoes

3.

A sick monk in the back row coughs
through the amen
The red candle behind him is made of wax
and a little string
Nothing to depend on, really, the squeeze-box
we call lungs
has only so many songs
Too short to see, Fr. Timothy's sweet voice floats up
for consideration — we all approve
if that matters
Who's holy here
would never know

4.

Compline: their last chance
and supplication to enter sleep
prepared
and mine, a guest here
to faith that anything can happen
For example, that the big orange cat
outside
without a name
another stray they feed
may protect us while we sleep
isn't, where God is concerned,
so far-fetched
Then the last monk the abbot blesses
blows out the candle

5.

The turnover, if that's what you call it,
is measured in simple crosses
made of wood
(all the same size)
in a row
by the east side of the abbey
The old monk who cooks the food
doesn't believe in the potato salad today
or in the tomato sauce he mixes
into the rice
He wants what they all want
the food to mean less
or more: Christ in the room,
the quiet to go deeper

6.

The monastery goldfish just *is,*
like zen to the community
in the pond behind the retreat house
the world has not fallen
farther than the three feet he swims in,
an orange bell
the water sometimes pulls
quietly
to the surface

7.

All the brothers turn out
for the photograph: abbot, priests,
the novitiate who, in the last war
might have been their navigator
Really a group shot
just before take-off
their hearts, "out there"
and sealed in prayer
for Our Lady of Guadalupe
In the background, open sky
and gray bell tower
announces Vespers
I especially love the eyes
of these Trappists,
old-world
with a bloom of innocence
for the earth
down here,
all squinting, now,
at the camera, into the sun

LAUDS

As much as anything
the song of the grey dipper
pulling the light
up stream

The candle that won't go out
barely lights the room
for monks everywhere
it is already late

I think of clay and how the dead
return to it
but not all at once

Whatever I want can wait
This is how I praise the morning
Giving in
my head down
on the yellow oil cloth

SECTION III

PRAYER

The best prayer is small, its eyes closed
In odor it resembles nutmeg

If it can fly at all it's like the blackbird
going out a few feet then back
to the bulrush.

The trades have prayers: for a roofer
a square of 3-tab means three bundles
weighing 80 pounds each, carried up
the long ladder, one at a time. It's dirty work.
Mostly you hear the grunts, the huffing
and Jesus Christ.

What does it mean to have a prayer life?
Hard to generalize. Sun. Water. Dirt — all gifts.
(Some people do)

The poor are more disposed to prayer. It's a train
they want to catch
Lots of bright, comfortable seats
A view toward the blue mountains
The food hot

But it's not very pretty to see
the prayer up close
the pale face pulled forward
and down. Affliction, the oldest painting,
untoward, red

A CHANCE TO TRAVEL

A wave is water
doing something
to the land and to all of us
The first sound we trust
curves in
to build a harbor

Doing something miraculous
is the verb
(He caused the loaves to multiply)
inside almost everyone
who would listen

ᭀ

The 10-hour work day
kills the spirit — in Europe
it's what the workmen call the trade
entering the body
Is that what you want?

∽

The Spitfire was the superior plane
over the Channel
and not the mush you hear about God
being on the side of the British
Prayer, it must be true, saves individuals
Never countries

Try to imagine the parachute
opening at night over the water
and the pilot, amazed, releasing himself
from the harness
still a 1000 feet up
(It happened all the time)

∽

Falling has no equivalent. It's a concept
that gives off distance. We like that. No more war
A chance, finally, to travel

THE WAR EFFORT, 1945

Everything right now is a reminder of the war I was
too small to fly in: green trees warming up in the
wind, the bus driver on the corner, a dead ringer for
my Uncle Benny, Army Air Corps, eagle wings
clutching a white star flying out of the blue patch
on his right shoulder, lost over the Pacific I
imagined. The old ache in my palm for the flyer's
45. Nights were dark. God wouldn't make my legs
grow any faster or give me a thin brown moustache.
You see, I loved America, and wanted to come
screaming out of the sun in more than balsa-wood
and rubber band. It was hard to throw myself into
the radishes and the potatoes, to believe in the dull
earth — that a little green garden could save us. All
the color was gone out of the giant, oily carp I'd
found, dead, lying across from the Buick factory
along the Flint River so close to where the night
shift riveted together the bright fuselages. I don't
know why I had to find it or how my colorless
uncle got so big in my mind. He molested my little
cousin and went, long ago, down the dirty river. It's
just that you make promises when you're a kid, to
eat everything, to the sidewalk up ahead that you're
coming, by God. Who can understand this country?
The surplus of feelings. The peace that never comes.

BOMBER PILOT

I don't hate him for it. He was a World War II
bomber pilot but wouldn't say more when I asked
him if he'd ever killed anyone. I loved the war the
way only a 12-year-old boy could in America, and
he was giving me a ride in his pickup out Wible
Road toward our place. It was a warm, sunny day in
Bakersfield. I could see the black dog way up ahead,
in the sun, on the road. I kept waiting for him to
slow down or for the dog to move. But neither did.
There were some little kids playing by the roadside.
One, in gray diapers, waved a chubby arm at me
when we went by.

Then we just ran over the dog, and there was
the clear thump through the running boards. Three
times. I looked back. The dog was lying in the
center of the road, kicking. The kids were watching
the dog. That's it. Nothing. He didn't stop. It
happened 35 years ago and I couldn't do anything
about it then or now. "I thought it would move,"
was all the bomber pilot ever said. After that I don't
remember anything: where he let me out, if he had a
moustache or not, the kind of pickup he drove.

For a long time I tried to make him into Richard
Widmark who flew B-17's in a movie I loved and
because, together, I imagined we would go back
there and change the outcome: it would be like the
film running backwards until the dog gets back up
on its feet. Then we enter, driving down Wible
Road. Widmark is shy but clear-sighted. We are

both concerned for the dog, out on the road like that, "It might get hurt," I say. As we approach, Widmark slows way down, then stops. He gets out and gathers the little dog into his arms. "Maybe we should knock on a couple of doors, find out where this guy belongs, Tom," or in another version, in his flight jacket, he steps out of the pickup and whistles to the dog. The dog somehow understands everything. That the road is no place for a dog.

You see, on Wible Road I had all this freedom. In the summer I didn't walk — I ran out the back door, the screen door slamming behind me, a peanut butter sandwich stuffed inside my shirt. Some days I must have walked 20 miles. Any direction was right. South was Paiute Packing Company and the stockyards where the fat cows always entered whole on the east side, up a long wooden ramp, but came out frozen and quartered on the west, over the backs of big men like my brother-in-law who loaded them into the long trucks at the docks. West was desert and oil wells. Everywhere there were animals: jackrabbits, hawks, coyotes. I hit a coyote once with my slingshot, right in the hip as he was loping by, so hard he did a complete somersault. It all happened so fast, it surprised us both. Then he was up and gone like it never happened. If I found some bones one week, a rabbit, a bird, in another week they were scattered. Nothing stayed. Not even the gray tumbleweeds which were especially fun to watch climb over each other and over the barbed-wire fences during sandstorms, then roll and bounce across Wible Road in front of the swerving cars. You felt like they knew where they were going. I lived on hunches. Walked backwards. Explored anything old I could get inside of. Adults were the worst thing that could happen to you because, around them, they made all the decisions. I only rode with the bomber pilot (he said he was a bomber pilot) because he offered and it was late and I was miles from home and hungry and I knew that my dad might boot me in the ass. He liked to say that, "You get moving Tommy or I'll boot you in the ass."

It wasn't unusual in those days, mostly farming country, for local people to offer you a ride. Besides, I was a kid. But he wouldn't tell me anything about the war, what kind of plane he flew even, and he ran over the dog. It was small, black. I remember that, and us bearing down on him. When I got Lulu from the Animal Shelter in Sacramento many years later I wasn't trying to change anything. I had a big yard, and we needed each other. That's all.

UNTITLED

The frustrated boy
chases a squirrel around
the trunk of a tree
assigned, already, a lesson
in mystery
he soon gives up
What we can't see, it turns out,
we walk away from

❧

Back in the woods
the mother deer watches me
pull her dead fawn off the road
It's an old story, though,
the stone hits the pitcher
and there is the usual mess
then someone appears
to clean up

❧

Asleep
I watched us
walking through a field of sunlight
my arm around your neck,
both crying the sweetest tears
and I'm telling you, "See Bill,
it's alright to die,
didn't I tell you."

❧

Dear life,
I told you I was weak,
almost fifty
the truth is
I have broken both of my arms
trying to lift you

AUTUMN

Think back when this time of year didn't have a
name. And dying was what it's always been, cold, a
damn shame. Moon of the red leaves meant
something don't you suppose, in the holy dark. And
geese, in their own sweet time, must have pointed
the way. That was before plastic and the phone
ringing off the hook. When feelings probably carried
the day. Or put another way, when the ice retreated,
we were warming up to the maple. It was time.
Evolution is the hand at rest, the distance from one
feeling to the next. Wives' tales. The paper
delivered almost to your door, skidding along the
walkway, coming to rest in a little puddle of rain
water. In time we will figure even that out and how
a tree can have us biting our nails, I mean bitterly,
for a clue.

For Ray Carver

SALMON

By now
two old fish,
you swim into the gravel bar
under the bridge
Aren't you, like us, looking
for the precise place
Now, where the thistles grow
there was a foundation
a bedroom

It's the oldest story alive
the wind and rain bring
the red leaves down to the creek
down to the water
and we love the falling
the water coming down
all day and night
while we sleep
while we are falling asleep

AUTUMN IN AMERICA

I've set the truth down
in front of me
on the table next to the milk
which says, if I don't stop this damn lying
(The price always drives up sadness)
I'll never get to our place
with its big red door
or see a tree for what it is —
light, brought to a boil
or, if you like, what the pole is
to the flag
when the wind blows a country,
waving its colors

The idea is to get down on the floor
with Olive
my thin black cat
who died on Tuesday
of leukemia, that lovely word,
the white army now everywhere
its own defeat
and say, yes, and thank you. It's autumn
my favorite time of year
when breakfast means something

America sits down to its newspaper,
the leaves we can all read
which say, it's awfully cold today
If you're going out wear a warm coat

You people in Salem, don't forget the dying
Tie your shoes

PUMPKIN

It's always the same,
no face will hold a candle
to the one you're carving
the one you'll hold up
against the old darkness of October,
cold night, the solitary man
in the moon is you
thumped on the head so many times
you have to be scared of yourself
and whatever else comes up
you couldn't look for
The sticky signature is all you get
from the years of aping yourself
now, only a rough translation —
Orange man
sad man
what pushes your hand is holy: stars,
goblins, seeds

DOGWOOD

You couldn't say dogwood
and mean an after-thought,
something God threw on
going out the door
a black tie for the poet
who loves the leafy tree
the darker one
back from the road
that blooms to high heaven
just to remind us
how energy plays. Bellflowers
strung together out of words
and the roots of words
right here, we might say
for the taking
where the road plays out
dogwood, an old invitation —
what colors wave us in?

IN PRAISE OF THE LIGHT

Light is better than an idea
It can pile up on the leaves to amaze us
or in moving away, never leave
It likes best the door ajar or the closed one
about to open
In restaurants, for example, it prefers the ordinary,
high ceilings
a worn red table near a window
Here we can sit alone and look down
calmly
while we examine, for awhile, our hands
around a cup of black coffee
and think about this country, our history, mostly
        sad
Where it's quiet we learn logic
doesn't hold a candle

꙾

When they say, "light enters a room,"
I think, Oh, I know a woman dead with salt and
        pepper hair
who will not leave me,
who will not leave this room for a minute
and that *must be* what they mean,
to hear a woman laughing
and to be reminded of trees when she enters
is to really love the light

꙾

My two cats play in the room,
a tabby and a black and white
You see, right away we are praising the light
that falls and falls around them
where they stretch out now asleep
on the kitchen floor

꙾

"We think she has a chance,"
he says, in a letter to his friend in Visalia,
"she points out the window again
and she recognizes some of her friends
and yesterday on the back porch, Bill, the sunlight,
she said, lifted her spirits."

꙾

Maybe in the end we will laugh anyway,
having made too much of the light
going and coming
while we sleep, as they say, our lives away,
your smooth right leg thrown over my left one
our heads hard together in the dark
Out of habit
we hold on
to each other's wonderful sex,
the rest, the dreams, we feel lucky if they are in
        color

THE FRANKLIN EXPEDITION 1855

Three feet down
and 130 years in the permafrost
didn't improve your sense of humor, William Brain
Like the guest of honor
you couldn't excuse yourself
from the party
in search of the Northwest Passage
or the frozen subsoil
which preserved your bulbous lips
in the shape of permanent disdain
Actually, in those latitudes, a winter smile
impervious to last rites
and the gnawing polar bear,
you just settled in

I'm watching the whole thing on television
from my gray couch
in the modern age
The archeologists recover your body
(It's all on film)
by pouring warm water over you_the thaw
you couldn't plan for
your eyes wide open and amazed
when they pulled back the wool blanket

Come here, Krissy, I'm yelling to my wife
in the kitchen
Come and look at *this*

This is what we do, now, to keep our interest
in death
cordoned off by little ropes then measured
down to the last blue homemade button
on your navy blouse
identified, finally, by a woman
they flew in from Newfoundland
Hell, it's an international event. Did we lose
        something
long ago, the way we stare back?
Forget some shortcut between two oceans
stalwart men and probable cause of death
The boats were made of wood, vulnerable, love
        letters
and we want them back:

"Dear William,

Devonshire is a long way from the Arctic. I expect
it's very cold. I miss you. Remember the first time
we made love? I know God approves and old Mrs.
Coates coming up the stairs, she almost caught us.
Wouldn't we have made a pretty picture together in
that empty room with all the sunlight? Just what
she'd expect of a sailor. Write your thoughts down
William, the way I told you. You're somebody too."

For Adrian and David

MARRIAGE

A fiction the cockeyed consent to
The "I do" of all great art
not in the object but in the design
that won't hold still
for as long as it takes
to pull together their history
or the knife through the ancient cake
while the camera records,
we are all gathered here together
in whatever film you're shooting
the lovers blur, paired,
like birds to build marriage
out of what has been lost,
a black shoelace, the fisherman's hoochie
or hair from the dead dog
Marriage, held open,
gives off a hundred wild odors
from the old streets which run
in all directions. Where nothing is new
Desire. Rain. In the windows, flowers,
always the sweet peas or marigolds
too heavy for their red pots
Marriage, that wants everything,
casualties, the poem, digging in
its blessing, unattainable song

SNOW

Snow doesn't say, "You win the new Oldsmobile, and you, you're fired." When it falls, it falls on all the houses. First leaflet, wing. We have to look up at this air, mottled and cold, a white handshake. And what could be friendlier to roof, fencepost or chicken than no preference — it supports all the arts. On war it comes down harder. Trucks can't get through. Guns jam. "Hell, we can't fight in this stuff," the General says, shaking his head. The black Lab, however, goes out in it, we imagine, to provide some contrast. It's not easy to follow just one white flake down all the way to the ground but it *is* restful and the poet should try. Try to see the humor, poor man, emotional at the wheel, going sideways down the street, taking out the red fire hydrant, and for what, bread and milk. It's the car that gives snow its bad name. It's man the snow can't trust to lie down and be covered.

THE HEART

The heart, we tell ourselves, is a pump
like any other
Some things are just true: the fist
we are asked to tighten
brings up the large vein
How much grief is enough?
Old Mrs. Vorhees
standing on swollen legs
on the front porch
waving at us, believe it or not,
with a red handkerchief. Now she's dead.
I don't know why we won't listen
If someone holds up a sign which says,
"You're next," we all look around
for the unlucky one
Aren't we numbered among the chosen —
what's measurable? The walk to the gate
before boarding. The solitary ride home.

MY FATHER'S HANDS

Because his hands were large, my father put a lot of stock by them. He was a carpenter and an inventor which meant he always had something in them: a tool, a board, a tape measure, and in the evening always a can of beer or a hard drink. His hands had a way of drawing attention to themselves . . . standing out. For one thing they were beautifully proportioned — long, muscular fingers with broad nails and longer by a full inch than his equally powerful palms. Tools, in particular, showed off his hands. When he gripped a hammer it meant something — one always complimented the other, both became one, larger now with something important to do. He seemed to know how important his hands were because he took good care of them. He washed them. Trimmed the nails regularly. Rubbed in large quantities of Lanolin. If he got a sliver in a finger, he took pains to remove it right away. His hands, their condition, was as important to him as any of his tools which he assiduously maintained. To protect the blade, planes were always laid on their sides. Saws — crosscut or rip — went into their wooden carriages, drill bits back into their oiled pouch. He seemed to understand that the condition of one determined the performance of the other. There was nothing he did that didn't require the whole participation of his hands. So it was odd, even humorous to watch him in the morning lift his delicate coffee cup and saucer, both dwarfed by the size of his hands, up to his lips and sip. Or when he danced solo, for example, which he loved to do, he would clap his hands and the strong fingers and thumbs would snap . . . the music was just another kind of tool his hands could explore, give shape to. In our family, "measuring up" in a real sense began with my father's hands. At least once a month he would spread one out in front of him in the air, usually his right one, full length for the three of us boys to compare to our own. Dickey, the oldest, would step up first. Then Billy. It was a ritual we looked forward to. A sure way, we believed, of seeing how we were doing. I was small for my age. So to hold up one of my hands to one of his hands (he called them his meat hooks) only exaggerated how far I had to go. And when he was mad I never saw the hand that cuffed me. He liked to say that when I did a job wrong: "You want me to cuff you." When he died years later in Lompoc I didn't go to the funeral. He was awfully thin, my mother said, from all the years of drinking. But the last time I saw my father was in a bar in Bakersfield. He was convinced that this little wooden instrument he had invented — a paddle in a box with springs on either side, that you play by holding in one hand and slapping with the other — that it was going to make us all rich.

KEEPSAKE

The boy is fifty-one.
Over the back of his hand
he can see the wrinkled skin of his father.
He throws the sheet off his legs
just like his father had done.
Even though they are his legs
the big calf muscles still startle him.
They remind him of the milk and crackers
he brought to his father in bed.
The fact is, he loves the old man,
dead twenty years now but
before that riding off
every night in a pulp Western.
So hard to figure dying: aging,
he begins to understand
is the only keepsake.

GRANDFATHER

This would be before the war when sweet butter
came from a wooden churn and no one had heard of
the word cholesterol. The way in is past the old hay
rake on the left, the iron seat with its 26 holes (I
counted them), is still sound if I want to ride back
to a field I could have sown anywhere: Sweet Home
. . . Chowchilla, USA. Red heads of barley wave and
rustle like a great sail in the afternoon wind, rolling
first one way, then the other, across 80 acres handed
down to me from my great grandfather, hog farmer,
Baptist, Populist. Sounds good, doesn't it? History
dreamy. From the front porch, looking down, at
least the field is accurate, except there was no wind
and it was wheat I rode through, astride a giant
horse named Billy. I was nine. I loved her, the smell
of her sweat that lathered up white around my legs
in the heat. The slow way she had of drinking water
at the trough after work, sucking it up through her
great yellow teeth that clicked sweetly the whole
time under those soft gray lips with the long hairs
on them. The trough lined in moss where beautiful
blue fish lived on the bottom. They were tiny in
among the gold motes. My nephew called them
Jesus fish because it was just luck if you saw one.
My grandfather was bitter so he didn't hand down
anything. He was small in his bib overalls and
looked like one of those rotted-out fence posts that
stands there only because the barbwire holds it up.
He took my penis out in a wheat field one day after

we'd eaten our lunch. You have to see me standing
there near Billy, the sun beating down and his big
hand pulling at my pants. I concentrated on her, on
the leather collar she had to wear with the brass
knobs I held on to, and the black straps that
followed the large curves of her body down over the
rump. Every evening he would hold up her hooves,
one at a time, while I dug out the hardpan packed in
around the frog. The thing is to remember Billy.
And if he's bad, don't say my grandfather doesn't
matter or that history stinks. You get the hay rake,
don't you, and the blackbirds coming in, ahead of
schedule, over the field we planted. What did you
want? A new backhoe? God in the poem? Some
barred-rocks running around?

WASHING

First of all Lord, thank you for the pumpernickel
and the liverwurst without which I could not
properly honor my mother who died as we both
know too soon, her head held under. "Dick," she
said to my father when I was nine, "you're an SOB."
She didn't stutter. Dark haired. German. She
smoked Pall Malls. Played the piano by ear. Had an
itch on her left arm that she said felt too good
scratching to ever let heal. Where does poetry come
from anyway: Stever Avenue in the backyard,
across from the Church of the Nazarene, where I
walked around the galvanized tubs, at five, trailing
my hand in the cold water? I really don't know. I
was in charge of the clothespins. The sheets coming
through the ringer. It's where I first discovered
longing. The sun going in and out. The sweet smell
of soap. All the sounds of the Maytag. Between the
earth and the clothesline, Lord, my mother ruined
me. Now I wouldn't trade for a whole war one white
pillowcase caught in the wind or for that matter a
pair of black socks.

Birds: murres (?)   p.29
        gull
herring gull   p.27
blue heron   p.32

You have beautiful eyes
she stood up
showing her little blue dress
    a little girl in St. Thomas Church
        Nov. 9. 2008

About the author

Tom Crawford was born in Flint, Michigan in 1939. He grew up in California in the Kern Valley. After graduating from Sacramento State University with a BA/MA in English, he taught for seven years, English and poetry writing, at Solano College in the bay area. His first collection of poems, a chapbook entitled, *I WANT TO SAY LISTEN*, was published by Ironwood Press. In 1987 Lynx House Press published, *IF IT WEREN'T FOR TREES*. In 1986 he received his second National Endowment for the Arts award. He lives with his wife, Krissy, in Hebo, Oregon.